How To Say No
And Keep Your Friends

How To Say No
And Keep Your Friends

Sharon Scott

First Edition, Eighth Printing,

Library of Congress Cataloging in Publication Data

International Standard Book No. 0-87425-039-0

For "the boys and the girls"
—the very special ten

ABOUT THE AUTHOR

Sharon Scott is a Licensed Professional Counselor, president of Scott and Associates, an international lecturer, and a frequent national and local radio and television talk show guest. Her Dallas-based firm offers training and consulting services to school districts, counseling agencies, law enforcement settings, religious groups, and parent and youth groups. With a master's degree in Human Relations and Community Affairs, she has developed many innovative programs during her 16-year counseling career. These include training adult sponsors and leaders of various peer groups in schools in developing student support groups to combat negative peer pressure. She has personally trained over 20,000 youth in her proven effective peer pressure reversal techniques.

Ms. Scott served as Director of the Dallas Police Department's First Offender Program. That program reduced recidivism from a base rate of 60% to a diversion rate of 20% for more than 10,000 youth, and became a national model for delinquency prevention and youth rehabilitation.

An authority on parenting skills, she is the author of *Peer Pressure Reversal—An Adult Guide to Developing a Responsible Child.* She has trained over 12,000 parents on topics such as building confidence, teaching responsibility, and peer pressure reversal. She writes a "Positive Parenting" column for numerous school districts' newsletters, and has conducted inservice workshops for thousands of teachers and counselors on topics including controlling classroom behavior and use of peer pressure reversal techniques in the classroom. She is also a featured speaker at numerous conferences including the PRIDE '86 International Conference on Drugs; American Association for Counseling and Development; Texas Police Association; Carolina Conference on Juvenile Justice; Texas Association of Non-Public Schools; Texans' War on Drugs; Texas Family Planning Association; and Texas Mental Health and Mental Retardation. Ms. Scott is the recipient of many awards for distinguished service to youth, including a Texas gubernatorial Certificate of Appreciation.

PREFACE

I had peer pressure decisions to make when I was growing up—whether or not to let someone copy my homework, whether to join in on gossip, let others choose my friends for me, how far to ride my bike away from home with friends, and later, where to take and not take the car, whether or not to drink alcohol, and many other frequently difficult decisions. And, like most young people nowadays, I worried about losing my friends if I didn't "go along" with the crowd. A big difference between you and me, though, is that you have to make those tough decisions at a much younger age than I did. Nowadays, kids are growing up very fast, which increases their difficulty in making decisions when their friends are teasing or encouraging them.

You can say no to trouble **and** be liked. This book covers many different styles of saying no when you need to—and being cool when you do! Read it carefully and add the things you like about it to your own style of dealing with your friends' negative peer pressure. It's serious at times and funny at times, but the main point is that you learn how to think on your own and make the right choices for **your** life.

There are several people I wish to acknowledge. They contributed much over the years to my education, training, career, and growth, and made this book possible. I am indebted to Dr. Robert Carkhuff, Dr. Tom Collingwood, Dr. Richard Pierce, and Dr. Bernard Berenson for encouraging and helping me to develop a strong skills base. My appreciation also goes to Lt. R.D. Wilson, Dallas Police Department, who developed the unique concept that led to the First Offender Program, where I first formulated my peer pressure reversal skills. I am also grateful to the counselors, past and present, who helped initiate then continued to operate that successful program. My special thanks to several who offered helpful suggestions: Dave Wagnon, toxicologist and a consulting teacher for drug education, my efficient secretary, Mary Lou McCoy, and, of course, the editors and publishers of this book. And a great big thank you to those young people who read and gave suggestions on my final manuscript: Chad, age 15, 9th grade; Nikki, age 15, 9th grade; Jeff, age 13, 7th grade; Carrie, age 12, 6th grade; Deborah, age 13, 8th grade; and Sarah, age 13, 8th grade.

June 1986   Sharon Scott
Dallas, Texas

TABLE OF CONTENTS

1.

INTRODUCTION

This book is about making decisions—**good** decisions. When you were young, your parents probably made all your decisions for you, from what you were going to eat to what you were going to wear. No doubt as you got older, you were given more opportunities to make your own decisions. As you enter your teenage years, you'll want to have the freedom to make your own decisions about friends, activities, school subjects, clothes, and so on. But in order to get that privilege, you'll need to have a history of making good decisions. As your parents start to think about giving you freedom to make more choices about your life, they will base their decisions on how well you've made decisions on your own.

You probably make many decisions every day: small, routine decisions such as what you are going to have for breakfast, what you are going to wear to school, and whether or not to pay attention in class. You have been making those kinds of decisions for years, and have probably become very good at it. There are other types of decisions—long-term decisions, such as college, career, and marriage. Those may take months or even years to think about. They require much serious thought.

This book is about a different kind of decision, called a **peer pressure decision**. It is a type of decision which may be the hardest of all for you to make, since (1) you'll have to think very quickly and (2) your friends or peers will be there trying to help you make the decision.

A peer is someone close to your own age. Pressure is not forced physical pressure in this case, but verbal pressure. It is things people say to try to encourage you to think as they think, or do as they do.

There is both positive and negative peer pressure. The positive kind can make you very happy about having friends. Positive peer pressure happens when someone encourages you to do your very best. Positive peer pressure is cheering your team on, talking a friend out of drinking at the party, or pushing friends to do their best in a difficult subject. Negative peer pressure happens when friends or acquaintances encourage you to do something that is wrong or dangerous.

You may think that nobody can force you to do anything you don't want to do. In a way, you are correct. Usually, no one forces you to do anything you don't want to do. The negative peer pressure discussed in this book is verbal pressure, when people tease you or put you down:

"Come on, it'll be fun, everyone is doing it."

"It's no big deal."

"Are you chicken?"

"If you were my friend, you would do this with me."

"Trust me . . . we won't get caught."

"I'll give you some money if you'll do this."

"I'm not going to invite you to my party if you don't do this with me."

"Be cool."

"You're a real wimp."

"What a nerd!"

"I dare you to do this."

"Nobody is going to find out."

"Grow up."

"You're a goody-goody."

I'm sure these are lines you have heard. They can easily get you into trouble.

Teasing or kidding can be hard to take, and sometimes you may want to go along with your friends to keep them, or just to get them off your back. If your friends use these peer pressure "lines" to try to get you to do something you shouldn't, and you let those lines get you involved, who is in control of you? Obviously, your friend is. If you knew you shouldn't go along and had no intention of doing so, but changed your mind because of the teasing, then your friend controlled you. Do you have any friends so brilliant and who know you so well that *they* should be making your decisions for *you*? Probably not! You know yourself best. You understand your family's values and what your parents expect of you. *You know what is right and wrong*, and therefore you should be making your own decisions.

It's sometimes hard to say no to friends when they want to borrow your homework; when they want you to stay out later than you are supposed to; when they want to go some place that could be interesting but dangerous; when they gossip or spread rumors about others; or when they are wanting to use drugs. You've probably faced decisions like these, and sometimes it's hard to stand up to your friends' pressures because you're afraid you won't fit in with the group.

We all want to be liked and to be popular. It's important no matter what your age. But if you think about it very carefully, it's possible to do both—have friends and be popular, *and* make good decisions and avoid trouble! **P**eer **P**ressure **R**eversal (PPR) is a method that will give you lots of ways to stop the pressure—to put it in reverse!—and get away from trouble.

Think about which of your friends it's hardest for you to say no to. Most likely you will think of best friends, the most popular group, older or bigger kids, and a boyfriend or girlfriend. This book will help you learn to get out of difficult situations, even with people that are really important to you. You will learn how to say no to trouble without offending others.

If a good friend asks you to do something you know is wrong, and you say "No thanks" and that person drops you, what kind of friend is that? It sounds to me like he or she might not be a real friend after all. That person might need to be the boss or the leader, and to call all the shots. If this person *really* is a good friend, how long will he or she stay mad at you for not going along? A few hours, or maybe a day? Can you live with a friend being mad at you for a day in order to make good decisions and stay out of trouble? I know you can!

I first got interested in how negative peer pressure can affect kids' lives when I was working with the Dallas Police Department, as Director of the First Offender Program. When I went to work for the police department, I knew that I would be working with young people, ages 10 through 16, who had made such poor decisions that they had actually broken the law and had been arrested. I thought that the type of kids I would be working with would act like criminals on TV, wouldn't know right from wrong, would have parents who didn't care, and would come from stressful home environments. I was surprised to find out that most of the kids who had been arrested—in Dallas, over 9,000 each year—came from loving homes, and had parents who really cared and had taught them right from wrong.

We observed that young persons taken into custody were scared, often crying, and unsure of what was going to happen next. Their parents were disbelieving and shocked when contacted. We started to examine carefully why these kids, who apparently knew right from wrong, had committed crimes such as burglary, shoplifting, substance abuse, driving while intoxicated, vandalism, skipping school, and many more. The single most important factor that influenced their poor decision making was negative peer pressure! Often these crimes were committed on a dare or a challenge.

Sometimes they were committed out of boredom, for "kicks"—when the kids felt they had nothing else to do. We saw kids—after they were arrested—arguing over whose idea it was to break the law. But it didn't matter: They had *all* broken the law and would *all* face the consequences.

Crimes committed by teens and preteens are on the increase across the country. Drugs and alcohol are available and in heavy use. Depression, unhappiness, and suicide are increasing. Poor decisions and getting in trouble are frequently causes of these problems, and being unable to handle peer pressure is often where all the trouble begins.

While I worked for the Dallas Police Department, I started to develop the peer pressure reversal techniques that are outlined in this book. They worked for the kids that were in the First Offender Program—80 percent of them *never* broke the law again. I have since taught these skills to over 10,000 kids—"normal," nice kids like you—who have found that these skills can give them lots of ways out of all kinds of difficult situations. These techniques of how to say no, but still be liked and be popular, will help you avoid tight spots, whether at home, in school, in your neighborhood, or any place else! You will learn up to ten different ways to handle peer pressure traps that may get you into trouble.

2.
STORIES OF
NEGATIVE
PEER
PRESSURE

Let's look at some real-life examples of what can happen when you make poor decisions while with peers. We'll examine how negative peer pressure can harm people physically, emotionally, and intellectually. These *true examples* are about kids of different ages I counseled over the years. Peer pressure can begin very young—in fact it starts in kindergarten. You have to make tough decisions at a very early age, much younger than your parents did. For example, it was probably not until their senior year in high school, if not later, that your parents first attended a party where alcohol was served. Many of you will encounter peer pressure involving alcohol and other harmful things in middle school and sometimes even in upper elementary school.

A boy in tenth grade played on the high school football team. He had always been a star player and had received much recognition in his football career. He also enjoyed many activities with friends—including parties—in high school. He soon learned that alcohol was available at a lot of the parties and occasionally marijuana was also offered. At first, when asked to participate in drinking and using drugs, he turned his friends down, saying he was trying to keep in shape for the football team. But as time went on he started thinking to himself that maybe his friends would think he wasn't cool if he didn't drink and smoke pot with them. So he started occasionally drinking "just one" beer, which led to more and more as time went on. Then he decided to try marijuana. Because of alcohol and drug usage, his body was not functioning as well as it used to, and he was having increasing difficulty concentrating on the plays during football practice. All of this started to become apparent during the football games. His coach started to talk to him about the way he was playing, and the boy quietly listened. But his friends were so important to him that he felt unable to stop using drugs, and even started getting high during the week rather than waiting for the weekend parties to come. *As he continued to make poor social decisions, his football skills deteriorated, and he got benched.* At that point he became so depressed his parents sought counseling for him. It was soon learned that alcohol and drugs were the cause of his problem, and that he needed to learn how to deal with negative peer pressure. When he became stronger in saying no to his friends, he found out that they would not cut him out of the group just because he didn't drink or smoke pot with them. I understand he played so well last season that scouts from many large colleges came to watch him play. In fact, he was selected as the best player at his position in his region!

A fourth grade student had dreams of being an astronaut. His father was an engineer and together they built model rockets. During the summer, this boy went to a camp for young people who were interested in aeronautics. Because of his ambitious goals, his grades were very important to him. He always got the highest grades in his class. He completed assignments on time, participated fully in his class, and would even offer to help the teacher. But some of the students in his class who were jealous of his grades teased him and called him the teacher's pet. No one likes to be teased like that, and when it began happening to him, he was confused as to how to handle it. At first he tried to ignore it, but when the teasing didn't stop, he started doing poor work in class so that he would be accepted by his peers. He was also very good at sports and games but was never chosen to be the leader. In this area, too, he began to slack off on purpose. When his next report card came out, his grades were lower than they had ever been. His parents were very disappointed, and when he explained why he had lowered the quality of his work, they realized he needed to learn how to deal with negative peer pressure. *In his case, negative peer pressure could have affected his entire life* and caused him to be much less than his potential—and his dreams. Once he learned the peer pressure reversal system outlined in this book, he learned how to keep his friends *and* reach his goals.

A thirteen-year old girl in her first year of middle school had recently moved with her family to a different state. When she began school, it was very important for her to meet new friends. Her parents both worked, and after school she was supposed to walk home from school and do her chores and homework, but she was not allowed to let friends visit during that time. One day, some of her new friends stopped by after school, and she stood on her front porch and talked to them for quite a while. They asked if they could come in, and she explained the rule at her home: no friends in until her parents came home. They continued to talk for a while and then left. The next week, this same group of friends stopped by and again invited themselves in. This time she did not feel quite as strong, and told them they could come in for just a few minutes. They said that was fine; all they wanted to do was talk and have a soft drink. After they got in, she was shocked to see that one of the kids had a bottle of alcohol and had started to mix it with the soft drinks. Not wanting to offend her friends, she went ahead and drank with them. They stayed quite awhile, but left before her parents arrived home from work. This started to happen on a fairly regular basis. She enjoyed their company and getting to know these new friends. At school they started to invite her to do other things, including skipping classes. One day she got caught doing this. Her parents were notified, and she was grounded for a period of time. However, she continued with the after school visits and drinking. Her parents did not know why she was slacking off on her chores and homework and became very upset with her when they arrived home and found she had not done the things she was supposed to do. She started losing more and more privileges and getting nagged a lot. Finally, her parents came home early one day and caught her drinking with her friends. She was severely punished and was forbidden to see those friends again. Her parents notified the friends' parents, and the friends were punished also. Again, *negative peer pressure caused loss of freedom* and forced adults to make decisions for someone who couldn't seem to make good ones by herself. But this thirteen-year old learned the information provided in this book. She learned to stay out of trouble while keeping her friends.

A fourteen-year old girl was also new in her school. She wanted to fit in so badly with the "in" group that she nearly forced herself on them. During the summer before school started, she made some friends in her own neighborhood, but they were not the most popular group and were not as important to her. As she continued to hang around with the "in" group at school, she found that a large part of their activities involved talking about others, and acting superior as though they were better than others. To try to fit in with this group, she would also gossip, even about the friends she had made during the summer. *Because she couldn't handle peer pressure, she began losing her real friends*, and was never really accepted by the "in" group. Another thing that happened was that her personality started to change from friendly and open to critical and conceited. She was not a fun person to be around. When she learned to deal with peer pressure, she went back to her real friends and kept the "in" group as casual, but not best, friends—and she was happy.

A sixteen-year old boy's parents left town on an emergency trip over the weekend. Since their son was going to be taking important six-week tests at school beginning the following week, they agreed to let him stay home and study. They felt that he was old enough to be left alone at home, and told him the rules of staying by himself, which involved checking in with the neighbors each evening, and not letting friends come into the house. While he was on the phone with friends soon after his parents left, he told them his parents were out of town. The friends got excited and said they would be right over to plan a party. He told them no, that he was not supposed to have company, but the friends said they were coming over anyway and hung up. When they arrived, he was not strong-willed enough to follow the rules, but let them in instead. The friends soon discovered the parents had left their sports car at home. They tried to talk this boy into driving them around in it, and he told them he did not have his license. They persisted, and he gave in. While showing off for his friends, he took a corner too fast and wrecked his parents' car. He was so upset at what happened, he tried to make the accident look as though someone had stolen the car and wrecked it. When his parents came back, that was the story he told them. The police were called. They investigated the situation, and discovered that the boy had wrecked the car himself. The parents were so frustrated by the many poor decisions their son had made in the past year—including skipping school, drinking, and cheating on homework—that they decided to send him to military school to learn discipline and responsibility. *Since he allowed himself to be influenced by his peers, he was not allowed to continue in the school of his own choice.*

The last true story of negative peer pressure is an extremely serious one about a fifteen-year old boy. During middle school, he was what some people might call an "all-American boy." He was a top student, had many friends, was quarterback of the football team, and got along very well with his parents. He was allowed to participate in a lot of activities and go many places because his parents trusted him so much. His family moved during the summer before he began high school, and he had to go to a school that very few of his former friends attended. He had to start making friends all over again. This bothered him, but he knew that he would fit in soon if he tried.

He began his first year of high school with his usual good grades and was also a star football player again. Everything was going well. But in selecting new friends, he had picked some of the older guys to hang around with. They looked and acted tough and also had cars, which was an extra advantage since he was not old enough to drive yet. He thought they were okay people, but soon found out they were involved in dangerous activities. They skipped classes now and then, and often asked him to join them. He always declined because he knew he needed to keep his grades up so he could continue to play football. Sometimes on weekends, when driving around with them, he noticed that they would speed and race, and though this concerned him, he never said anything. Frequently they had beer in the car, and offered him one, but he declined because he wanted to stay in shape for football. Sometimes they would even smoke pot, but when they invited him to try some, he turned them down.

As he continued to hang around with these guys, and they continued to pressure him to participate in these dangerous activities, he started to give in to some of their requests. He once skipped sixth-period class with them and didn't get caught. That gave him an excuse to try it again. On weekends he started drinking a little with them, and before long he was doing all sorts of dangerous things. He was afraid that his friends would think he was a wimp if he didn't go along. (A lot of the time, once someone makes one poor decision with friends, those friends expect that person to give in even more often.) He eventually got kicked off the football team because of his lack of interest, lower physical capability, and his poor grades. When that happened, he told the coach that he didn't want to play on the team anyway—that they weren't a good team. He was not only lying to the coach; he was lying to himself. He started staying out late with the guys and his parents got angry at him. He even started dressing differently. His parents tried discussing his selection of friends with him, and he would yell: "Get off my back. These are my friends. I like them; you can't choose my friends." But instead of things going well in his life, everything seemed to be falling apart.

He and three friends were driving around several weeks before Christmas. They were drinking, smoking pot, and griping about not having enough money to buy Christmas presents. The seventeen-year old driver suggested half-jokingly that they rob a convenience store and split up the money. They all took another sip of beer and joked that it was a good idea; they could probably get a lot of money. They all felt it was a good joke and continued to talk and laugh about this crazy idea that the driver had.

After driving around for a while and putting more alcohol and drugs into their systems, the driver pulled up at 1:00 a.m. in front of a convenience store, and said to his three buddies, "Look, there's only one guy inside. This will be easy; let's rob this place." The three others in the car said, "Hey, man, we were just kidding. We're not into anything this big. This is too much." The driver called his friends cowards. They all said they weren't scared. He looked at the fifteen-year old and said, "You come in with me and help. You other two stay in the car and watch for anyone driving by. If you see anyone, honk the horn so that we can get out of the store." The fifteen-year old, not wanting to be called a coward again, got out of the car and walked into the convenience store with the seventeen-year old. At first they were uncertain what to do; they went over to the video games and started playing them. Finally, the seventeen-year old walked over to the clerk and said, "This is a hold-up. Give me all the money from your cash register." The clerk reached under the counter for a weapon, and when he did, the seventeen-year old opened his jacket, pulled out a gun (that none of his friends had known about) and shot the clerk at very close range. The clerk fell to the floor with blood gushing from his chest. The seventeen-year old raced out of the store, jumped into his car with the other two friends, and sped away—leaving the fifteen-year old inside. He panicked; he didn't know what to do. All he could think about was getting home. He lived about two miles from the store, and he dashed out the door, leaving the bleeding man inside.

Soon someone arrived at the store and found the clerk bleeding behind the counter. They called an ambulance and the police. The clerk was taken to the hospital, barely alive. The police started investigating, talking with anyone who might have seen something to give them a clue about the crime. They happened to talk to a man who lived near the convenience store, who came home late from work that morning. The man told the police he saw a local boy running down the street. He told them that the boy was a good boy, and surely hadn't been involved, but perhaps he had seen something. He gave them the boy's name and address. The police went to the house and knocked on the door. The parents answered the door, and the police told them that their son was out late, and that he may have been a witness to an armed robbery. They asked to talk to him. The parents agreed and woke their son. When they told him the police were there, the boy became hysterical. His parents knew then that not only was their son a witness, but that he must have been involved in the robbery. He was arrested, as were his three friends.

All four of the boys were charged with attempted murder, possession of drugs, drinking under age, and robbery. All four of *these boys suffered severe consequences, including a lengthy prison term for the seventeen-year old (he was an adult under Texas law). The others were placed in juvenile detention. They were sentenced to counseling and long-term probation.*

The clerk spent many months in the hospital, but did survive. He was injured so severely that he will never be able to work again, and he now supports his family on a disability income. His life was ruined, as were those of the four boys, who now all have police records.

Notice in this situation that the fifteen-year old boy changed in three months from a good, reliable kid to one who would break laws! Whose fault was it that he changed? His friends'? No—it was *his* own fault. His friends didn't *make* him do wrong—they only asked him to join them. How could this story have ended differently? If the boy had said no to the idea of the robbery and asked to be dropped off at home—if he had said no to the alcohol and pot—if he had said no to skipping school—and, of course, if he had originally selected better friends. Unfortunately, he learned the peer pressure reversal techniques described in this book too late to help him in this situation. But he knows them now and is in the process of finishing his education.

Saying no to trouble ideas is not always easy. The following is a fictional peer pressure example; all the others in the book are true.

Sylvia Snob, Walter Wimp, Chuck Cool and Christine Confident are invited to a party at a friend's house on a Friday night after the football game. They assume it will be a party where no alcohol is served and that there will be adult supervision.

Each one is surprised by what is going on when he or she arrives. Each is greeted at the door by class-mates who are staggering and have slurred speech; they have obviously been drinking. As each one walks into the house, he or she notices the room is dimly lit. The party appears to be rowdy—a lamp has been knocked off a table. They see beer cans on the floor, and notice a group of kids huddled in a corner passing a joint around. They also notice that there are no adults at the party.

When Sylvia arrives at the party, she walks in and says loudly, "I can't believe this! I didn't know you were all drug addicts and alcoholics. I'm certainly not staying at a party like this. Good-bye!" She huffs out, slamming the door behind her. Sylvia has gotten out of the trouble situation, but in a way that may cause her tremendous teasing and kidding by that group of kids, and probably even by her closest friends. She handled the peer pressure trouble so strongly that it may cause others to think of her as stuck-up—and she is actually a very nice person.

A short time later, Walter arrives. His eyes get big as he walks in and notices all the trouble taking place.

He thinks about the fact that he could be arrested by being involved in a situation where alcohol and drugs are being used. Walter is undecided as to how to handle this situation, so when he walks in, he finds a corner to sit in, hoping he will not be noticed by his peers. However, someone soon comes by and offers Walter a beer. He replies in a soft voice, "I have never drunk alcohol before. I don't *think* I should now."

The peer replies, "Come on, Walter, it's no big deal. Everybody is drinking. Nobody is going to get drunk." Walter decides to try just a little, and then becomes fully involved in the trouble situation. He didn't make his own choice, so his friends chose for him. Walter had better be prepared for the consequences he will face because of his poor decision.

A while later, Chuck arrives at the same party. Chuck thinks he is so cool that he can even go to dangerous places and handle them easily. He thinks just because drugs and alcohol are being used at a party doesn't mean he has to join in. He's right, but if the party gets busted, even he would be in trouble. How would Chuck explain to his parents that practically everyone at the party was drinking and smoking pot but him? How would he explain this to the police? If he remains at the party, there is only one person who can pressure Chuck Cool: himself. His friends can't pressure him—if they offer him a drink, he'll probably reply, "I'm on the football team; trying to keep in shape. No thanks." But people like Chuck begin to think after a while, "Maybe no one thinks I'm cool at all—they may think I'm a wimp. I'll just have one." People like Chuck can pressure themselves into trouble!

Do you want to be a person like Sylvia or Walter or Chuck? Let's look at the fourth person who arrives at this same party, Christine Confident. Christine quickly recognizes that trouble is going on, and begins thinking about how she can get out of it. Christine would like to stay at the party with her friends, but knows there is too much of a risk if she does. Christine also knows that there will be other times to visit with these friends and many other parties to come. So after being at the party for just a few minutes, Christine might say something like: "Just wanted to come by and say hi. I sure wish I could stay, but I've got other plans. See you guys at school." Christine leaves the party calmly and drives home. (If Christine is not old enough to drive, then she could call a parent for a ride, or walk home. Or, Christine could always stay at the party for a short while and then say: "I don't see John; I'm gonna go check on him. I'll be back." And she could just leave the party.) There are many ways to handle a situation like that without being a snob, or a wimp. The point is thinking and acting quickly, like Christine did!

The next section will outline a proven effective way to handle peer pressure so that you can make good decisions and avoid trouble without damaging your friendships. Over 20,000 other young people have learned how to do this using the method in this book.

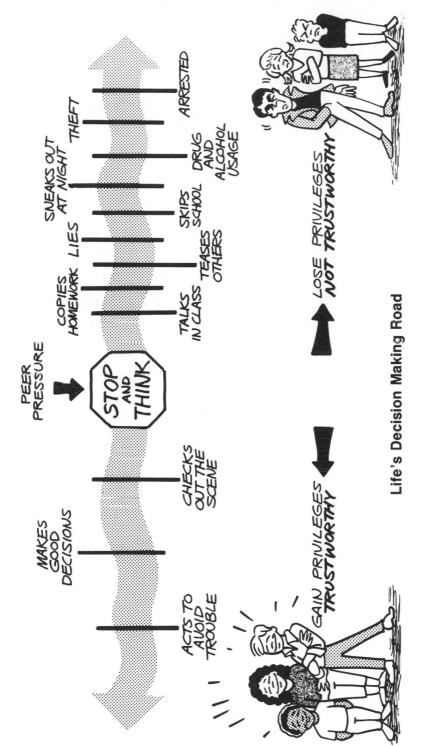

Life's Decision Making Road

3.

LEARNING PEER PRESSURE REVERSAL

So that you can avoid difficult situations and have the freedom to make your own decisions, let's look at a simple three-step skill called Peer Pressure Reversal (PPR). These three steps are guaranteed to get you out of tough situations, but let you continue to be a part of your peer group.

1) Check Out the Scene
2) Make a Good Decision
3) Act to Avoid Trouble

None of these steps is difficult, and they contain plenty of good common sense. Basically, the steps involve learning to identify potentially difficult situations. As a result, you'll be able to understand that the situation leads to certain consequences and take appropriate action to protect yourself. Learning these three steps will help you get out of the toughest peer pressure situations. You'll be more aware of what is going on around you, and you'll therefore use better judgment so that you can make more responsible decisions. When that happens, your parents will give you the opportunity to make more decisions *on your own*!

Step 1: CHECK OUT THE SCENE

This first step tells you to open your eyes, ears, and mind to what is going on around you. In a way, you need to become a "trouble detective." If you learn to pay attention well enough, you may be able to recognize trouble before it actually happens, so that you can avoid it entirely. It is important to realize very quickly when trouble is going to happen—or is actually happening—because you'll have to move fast. If you don't, you are likely to get tricked into the trouble, and no one wants to be a sucker! **Check Out The Scene** involves two parts:

A) Look and Listen

B) Ask Yourself: "Is This Trouble?"

LOOK AND LISTEN

If you get this part down, you'll be more aware of your environment, and what your friends are doing. You need to observe your friends (or the people with you) closely and notice if there is anything unusual or weird in the way they are grouped, acting or behaving. You should also look at the environment around the group. Are your friends in a dangerous place or set-up, such as an abandoned house or apartment; a party with no adult supervision; a deserted street or school; a dark building; or a situation that involves kids a lot older than you? You should also listen carefully to what people are saying. Listen for any hints or hidden suggestions. You must understand what they may be asking you to do, even though they are not putting their suggestions into words. Notice if your friends are speaking in an unusual manner. Are they trying to persuade you by bribing you? Are they blackmailing you with their friendship? Are they calling you names or threatening you? You also need to notice their tone of voice and be aware of anyone acting secretive. You want to be able to notice invitations to trouble that include very common peer pressure lines mentioned earlier, such as "Everybody does it," "We won't get in trouble," "It's no big deal," "Be cool," "Come on, grow up," "You scared?" and so on. *All of these lines can spell trouble for you*. Lines like these are never used to suggest an activity that is okay. Have you ever heard someone say to a friend: "Let's play football. We won't get caught. Everybody does it! It's no big deal." Those types of lines are unnecessary unless the suggestion is *trouble*.

Let's pretend you see a crowd gathering beside your school at the end of the day. You hear someone say "C'mon—hit him!" If you use the *look and listen skills* you would be aware that a fight is going to happen. Many people would go nearer to see more and might even become involved—not a smart thing to do!

Or, imagine you are walking home in your own neighborhood after visiting friends. A block ahead, you see some of your friends hanging around under a street light. You start to cross to their side of the street to say hi, when all of a sudden you hear glass break. The street light goes out, and you see your friends laughing and running in different directions. Do you run to catch up with your friends, and ask them what is going on? I hope not, since you should be able to recognize that what happened spelled trouble. The street light had just been broken by your friends. If you go to talk with them and someone saw what happened, you could be accused of having broken the street light.

The point is that if you see trouble coming before it happens, you can take appropriate action to avoid it.

ASK YOURSELF: IS THIS TROUBLE?

This is the second step of **Check Out the Scene**. Sometimes when a friend asks you to do something, you may not be sure if it is wrong. If you ask yourself: "*Is this trouble?*" you will be able to consider whether or not you should avoid the activity. Ask yourself: *Does it break a law or will it make an authority angry*? If after thinking it over (even for a second) you can answer yes to that question, then you are definitely facing a trouble situation.

The first half of asking yourself "*Is this trouble?*" is "Does it break a law?" Whether or not you believe a law is right or fair, breaking it can bring severely unpleasant consequences. You could get arrested, be fined, be extremely embarrassed, get put on probation, and so on. Young people can do many things that break the law: stealing, skipping classes, drinking while under the legal age, using marijuana or other drugs, burglary, assault, drunk driving, carrying weapons, arson, and vandalism.

The second half of asking yourself "Is this trouble?" requires you to think about whether what you are being asked to do will make someone in authority angry. Some examples of authorities are: parents, teachers, principals, coaches, neighbors' parents, shop owners, police, activity leaders, employers, and so on. If your family is religious or spiritual, you might also think of a "supreme being" as an authority figure. No matter what your age, there are authority figures in your life that you do not want to anger. There are many things that can cause a person in authority to be angry, including coming home late (this will anger your parents), not doing your best on your homework (this will upset your teacher *and* your parents), or stealing (this will anger the store owner, police, and your parents).

One universal law of human decency is that we should treat others the way we want to be treated. If you are selfish or unkind, and if you are thoughtless to others, that could anger people who can put restrictions on your activities. Asking yourself: "Is this trouble?" is already a good indication that there may be trouble if you get involved in the activity.

Listed below are five social situations. You need to ask yourself "Is this trouble?" for each of these five examples, and answer yes or no.

1) While your parents are gone the dog gets out. Rather than running to get her, you take the car, even though you don't have your drivers license yet.

2) Your parent drops you off at the movies but you change your mind after your parent drives away, and decide to go walking around someplace else.

3) You go to a slumber party and at midnight, because there is nothing good on TV, you walk up and down the street for some fresh air with your friends.

4) You attend a chaperoned party with a lot of your friends. You dance the evening away but make it home on time.

5) You and a friend buy a soft drink at your local grocery store. Your friend then takes some candy. You tell your friend to put it back but he doesn't. You leave the store together.

Of the five examples, only the fourth does not involve trouble. Each of the others will either break a law or anger an authority figure. Number 1 will upset your parents and the police. Number 2 will cause your parents to be upset because you changed plans without asking their permission. It could even be dangerous—

no one would know where you were if anything were to happen to you. Number 3 will anger the parents of the friend you were staying with, as well as your parents if they are called. If your town has a curfew, you could be breaking a law. Number 5 would anger your parents and the store owner. Stealing is against the law, and even though it was your friend and not you who took the candy, you would be considered an accomplice in a shoplifting charge.

The first step in peer pressure reversal, **Check Out the Scene**, allows you to be more aware of what's going on around you and to recognize potential trouble.

Step 2: MAKE A GOOD DECISION

The second PPR step is: **Make a Good Decision**. After you've noticed that a situation is one that can lead to trouble, this PPR step actually pushes you to make a choice. It makes you consider and understand the negative consequences that could result if you make a particular decision. It requires using your common sense and taking a few seconds to choose whether you want positive or negative results for yourself. It is easy to get caught up in the emotional charge of a peer's invitation to trouble. When friends excitedly tell you everyone is going to be at a planned activity, that it's no big deal, and that you won't get caught, it's easy to forget that it may indeed be a big deal, that you really *could* get caught, and that you could get into trouble. In order to **Make a Good Decision,** there are two things to think about:

A) Weigh Both Sides

B) Decide: Stop or Go

WEIGH BOTH SIDES

So that you can make an intelligent decision for yourself, you need to consider *both sides* of the situation. Ask yourself: "If I do this, what good can happen?" and, "If I do this, what bad can happen?" Actually, all you really have to think about is one side of the situation—no doubt your friend will tell you all about the other side. They'll tell you all the *good* things that might happen. But most likely, your friend won't tell you the bad things that are likely to occur. They'll build up the positive side. In order for you to make a responsible decision, you have to rely on *yourself* to consider the negative consequences, even though they might not happen. There is a very good chance that they *will* happen. Negative consequences could be: disappointing your parents and perhaps losing their trust; having your privileges taken away; losing good friends; getting nagged by your parents or teachers; having to serve detention; getting embarrassed; getting physically hurt; being arrested; and also damaging your own self-respect. If you carefully examine both the positive and negative consequences of a difficult situation and are really honest with yourself, you will find that the list of potentially unpleasant consequences is usually much longer. The risks involved are usually not worth going along with your friends.

For instance, imagine you are asked by a friend one afternoon to skip the last period of school. Your friend tells you there is a substitute teacher who is not checking attendance, and that it is no big deal. She suggests going to her house and having a soft drink. If you **Check Out the Scene** then you'll recognize potential trouble. You now *weigh both sides*: you wouldn't have to go to the class, you would get to have a soft drink with your friend, and you might have some fun. Then you should consider the bad things that could happen if you skip class: you could get caught by a teacher or the principal as you leave school, get punished, and have your parents called, and your parents would probably also punish you. You could also get caught by your friend's parents, and both sets of parents might agree that you and your friend were not to see each other any more. You could miss a class assignment. You could get picked up by the police for skipping school. Obviously, the list of negative consequences is much longer than the positive.

Pretend you have gone to your friend's house for the evening. His parents have ordered a pizza, which you and your friend are beginning to eat. Your friend's parents have to leave for about an hour to run some errands, and they leave the two of you there with your pizza. As soon as they leave, your friend goes to the refrigerator and asks if you want a beer. He tells you there are quite a few and that his parents never keep track of how many there are. Your friend tells you the beer is their favorite brand and really good. **Checking Out the Scene** will allow you to notice the potential for trouble here: drinking a beer with your friend breaks a law and could get an authority mad at you. If you were to *weigh both sides* of the situation, you'd probably realize that the good that could happen would be a fun time with your friend and, perhaps, feeling grown-up. The bad things could include getting caught by your friend's parents, who would probably talk to *your* parents and send you home. Your parents might ground you for a while. Or, you could drink too much, and get sick. You would be harming your health. After weighing both sides, you would realize that drinking beer with your friend is not a good way to appear grown-up and mature. It would show instead that you can't make your own decisions, and that you can be controlled easily by your peers.

DECIDE: STOP OR GO

Now that you have looked at both sides of a situation you need to *decide* which way you'll act. Do you want to avoid the trouble or risk it? You must choose one. It's important for you to know that if you do *not* make a firm decision, it will be very difficult for you to avoid the trouble. You will appear unsure and hesitant and open to manipulation (remember Walter?). You will not appear strong and confident in your decision, and this may cause your friends to apply more pressure and teasing to try to get you to go along. So you have to decide *clearly* whether it is worth it to participate in the activity. Should you decide to risk trouble, thinking, "Oh well, I won't get caught" or "So what if I do, it's not gonna be the end of my life," then be prepared to face the consequences. (In other words, don't do the crime if you can't do the time!) The consequences may lead to adults making more decisions for you and allowing you to make fewer yourself. If you risk trouble, you are risking a loss of freedom.

And there is always a chance you will get caught. If you imagine what the consequences would *really* feel like should you choose to go along with a friend, then you will be more determined not to take the risk. Not only will you have avoided negative consequences, but you'll probably feel good about doing the right thing: what *you* think is right.

Another thing that often happens when you decide against risking trouble is that your friends will be less likely to go ahead and risk the trouble alone. The only way your friends will go ahead alone is if they find someone else to manipulate. It can give you a good feeling to know that when you **make good decisions**, you not only help yourself, but a lot of the time you help your friends as well! You can actually become *more* popular in your neighborhood or school because you're strong, self-confident, and you set a good example. You might even be helping other kids stay out of trouble! In many school districts I have trained student peer groups who then act as leaders and helpers in their schools.

Let's say you are at lunch with a group of your friends, talking about a new girl in school. Some of your friends don't like her for one reason or another— maybe they think she is stuck-up. You have to make a decision about whether you will go along with your friends and put this girl down or whether you are going to give her a chance. Should you decide to give the girl a chance, you have just made the decision in your mind. You have made a confident decision to avoid a trouble situation.

Pretend you are spending Saturday night over at a friend's house and you're in his room talking and playing music. The evening looks like it is going to be fun until your friend suggests the two of you call up some kids from school and hassle them by making prank phone calls. If you decide *then* that this is a trouble situation (it could hurt people's feelings or even scare them, and could anger parents and even break the law!), then you have made a *decision* to stop and avoid trouble. Again, it takes confidence and strength to make good decisions consistently, but at some point in your life you *must* decide who is going to make your decisions for you. Will it be your friends, or yourself?

Step 3: ACT TO AVOID TROUBLE

This is the most important of the three PPR steps. The first two steps have prepared you for this step. Now you need to know *what to say or do* in order to stay away from or get out of the situation. Your goal is to avoid being manipulated. You must act constructively, and you will need a variety of responses so you can reverse peer pressure situations skillfully. You must be comfortable with these responses, too; you *can* reverse peer pressure without losing your friends or being teased. You can even build respect and admiration from your peers.

These responses are quick, clever, and effective. In this step you will learn ten responses. At least one or more should work for you. Sometimes it can seem like a battle out there, and these steps will allow you to win the "war" without hurting yourself or others. The two parts of **Acting to Avoid Trouble** are:

A) What to Say

B) How to Say It

WHAT TO SAY

Below are the ten peer pressure reversal responses. You often will use more than one to get out of a trouble situation. The ten choices let you get the friend away from the trouble or get *yourself* away from the friend. Having these choices can be just like getting rescued from trouble.

1. Just say no
2. Leave
3. Ignore
4. Make an excuse
5. Change the subject

6. Make a joke
7. Act shocked
8. Flattery
9. A better idea
10. Return the challenge

Why so many choices? Because you are different ages and have different personalities. Each of you will find techinques that you prefer. Be looking for which responses will be best for *you*. Now let's look at these responses one by one.

1. JUST SAY NO

In this basic PPR response you just say *NO*. It is an upfront, honest, direct, and courageous choice. It is simple and effective. It can be done politely or firmly— depending on how much pressure you're under. The key to doing this is to keep it short and closed to further discussion. Your voice and facial expression can tell your friends exactly how you feel about their pressure.

You can probably think of other ways to say no; here's a start:

Shake your head.
"No thank you."
"Don't feel like it."
"Thanks, but no thanks."
"Don't think I will."
"I'll pass."
"I'm not really
  interested."
"No way!"
"Definitely not."
"Not if I want to live."
"That's wrong."
"Can't."

"Uh-uh."
"I'd rather not."
"That's dumb."
"Don't want to."
"I don't think so."
"Next year—remember to
  ask me then."
"Are you crazy?"
"Nope."
"Not if I want to see
  tomorrow."
"Forget it!"

You can also use the "broken record" approach by repeating the same phrase over and over until your friend gets the message and gives up. For example, if your friend suggests that you ride bikes to an off-limits area, you say, "I'm not interested." As your friend continues to beg, you keep saying, "I'm not interested" until he or she takes the hint.

2. LEAVE

You might just walk away from the trouble situation. If you are in a group, they may not even notice if you leave. If it is just you and another friend, you might choose this response if you can't think of anything to say or just don't want to continue arguing with your friend. You don't even have to explain yourself; actions speak louder than words.

It is important *how* you leave a trouble situation so that you avoid further teasing. You must try to walk away with a confident attitude. You can even walk off casually, shaking your head a little, as if you can't believe what your friend just suggested, or wave your hand at your friend as you walk away like that was the silliest idea you had ever heard. It is important that you *leave* the area completely and do not return any time soon, or else your friend may begin pressuring you again.

This technique can also be used at another time to stress your seriousness about refusing your peer's suggestion. If a friend has asked you to do something you don't want to do and you have used several other PPR techniques with no success, the only alternative is to *walk away*. The rule is that you say no, in any PPR words, *no more than twice* before you walk away. If you continue arguing with your friend, one of two things could happen: You could get talked into the trouble, or, you could get into a serious argument with your friend. The best idea is to get out of trouble situations quickly.

3. IGNORE

Another PPR technique is to *ignore* your friend's comment or suggestion. You can appear to be busy studying, listening to music, deep in thought, distracted by what someone else is saying—just don't listen to what your friend is saying. This response is great in class when a peer is trying to get you to talk, pass homework or notes, show test answers, etc., because at these times if you say something, even "Shh, we're not supposed to be talking," you could get caught by your teacher just at that moment. On the other hand, if you *ignore* your friend, he or she will either give up and try someone else, or get caught (instead of you!) by the teacher. Choosing to *ignore* can be used easily in a situation where gossip and rumors are being discussed—perhaps while you are riding the bus home from school. You can pretend to be reading or start packing up your things to get ready to get off the bus. The next day maybe you could make an effort to sit elsewhere on the bus to avoid a repeat problem with the same friend.

4. MAKE AN EXCUSE

This way of handling peer pressure seems to be most teenagers' number one choice. *Making an excuse* is thinking of something you could or should be doing instead. Try to base your excuses on the truth, even if exaggerated, because if you just lie you probably won't sound convincing, and your friend could catch you later in that lie and be really mad at you. Also, lies can lower self-esteem. *Making an excuse* can be vague: "I don't feel like it," or very specific: "I've got to go home and study." The important thing is that you come up with a reason to get away from the invitation to trouble. Some examples of good excuses are:

"I've got to go home and do my chores. I didn't do them yesterday and I'll really get in trouble if they're not done today."
"I just got off being grounded and I don't plan on taking any risks now."
"I've got to go study for a test."
"I've got a book report due."
"My parents would kill me!"
"I have to go to practice _____ ." (piano, soccer, football, dancing, etc.)
"I've got to babysit my brother."
"I need to help with dinner."
"I'm expecting a phone call."
"I've already got other plans."
"I'm tired."
"I don't feel like it."
"I'm not in the mood."
"I *always* get caught. Take me along and we'll all get in trouble."

There is one excuse that never fails: "I don't feel well. I've got to go to the bathroom." Then take your time in the bathroom in order to give your friend time to leave!

5. CHANGE THE SUBJECT

When a peer suggests trouble, you could choose to *change the subject*. This involves quick thinking and fast talking. In order to *change the subject* convincingly, you must pick a topic that will get their interest or take them by surprise. Some good examples are:

"Guess what John said about you; it's all over school." Your friend will probably be surprised and ask, "What did he say?" Then you answer something like this: "He said you're really cute." Now you know what you and your friend would be talking about—not the trouble situation!

"What are you going to wear to the dance next month? I haven't decided yet, have you?"

"I really like your shoes. Where did you get them?"

"Did you watch the game Sunday? Four interceptions, wow!"

Once you have got your friends to discuss a new subject, you need to keep them there so they won't return to the pressure situation.

6. MAKE A JOKE

If you have a good sense of humor, then this technique is for you! Coming back with a *joke* can be a funny *and* effective way of handling negative peer pressure. It can lighten the atmosphere and your friends will like it. Making your friends laugh can encourage them toward your way of thinking. You don't have to be a master comedian like Johnny Carson or Eddie Murphy. Just develop some fun, playful responses. Although a few of these examples will seem a bit corny, they can all be effective.

When you're asked to go somewhere you shouldn't, say. . .

"I'd love to, but I've already made plans. I've got to go home and rearrange my sock drawer."

"Rats, that's the same night as my Hollywood screen test."

"Love to, but it's my night to brush my dog's teeth."

"I wish I could, but I've got to walk my goldfish."

"I'd like to, but I need to spend more time with my plants. Sorry."

When you're asked to do something you shouldn't, say. . .

"Yeah, and right after that, we'll blow up Russia."

"Are you kidding? If I did that, my reputation might improve."

"I'm taking flying lessons; got to go meet my pilot. Bye."

"I've got to go call the Guinness Book of World Records. You just came up with the dumbest idea I've ever heard!"

"I just got a new pet. He's grey, weighs two tons, and has a long trunk. I have to water that sucker every five minutes, and it's time to do it again."

"NASA's expecting me to look at some moon rocks. I'm an expert on that subject, you know."

Another way of joking your way out of trouble involves "playing it dumb." When a friend suggests trouble, say, "I'm sorry, I don't get what you are talking about. What is it you want to do?" Your friend will probably explain it again more carefully. When he or she gets through, say, "I am really confused. What is it exactly you want to do? Explain it slower this time." A patient friend may go through it once more, at which time you say, "This just doesn't make sense. I don't understand exactly what you want to do or why. I think you are going to have to go through it one more time." At this point your friend will no doubt feel frustrated and say, 'Oh, just forget it." Instead of "playing it dumb," in reality you played it *smart* by frustrating your friend into giving up.

Be creative—I know you can make up funny comebacks on your own! Send me your ideas!

7. ACT SHOCKED

This technique allows you to act as if you can't believe what your friend has just asked you to do. You act amazed, astounded, as if you are in a state of shock! If this is a close friend, it gives you a chance to embarrass him or her by making it known just how wrong you think the suggestion is. Look at your friend and roll your eyes, let your mouth drop open, and say something like:

"I can't believe what I just heard. Do you know how much trouble you would get into? I won't let you even discuss it!"

"I know you didn't mean that!"

"I can't believe you even suggested that!"

"Oh sure! Just what I always wanted to do."

"You didn't really say that, did you? There must be a ventriloquist in the house."

"How silly! Earth calling *(your friend's name)*."

"How childish! How did I pick such a crazy friend? Just lucky, I guess."

"Where do you get your ideas? You must watch the Looney Tunes on Saturday morning."

You might be surprised, but these lines usually make friends back off and say something like, "Oh, I was just joking," or "I really wasn't serious; I just wondered what you thought about it."

8. FLATTERY

Flattery can get you somewhere—right out of a tight spot! Saying kind, thoughtful things about your friend often works beautifully to your advantage. Most of us don't get enough compliments anyway, and everyone is happy to hear *flattery*. And again, you not only help yourself to avoid trouble but you also help your friend. Obviously, you must tailor your *flattery* to the individual situation, but some examples are:

"You're too smart to really mean that."

"You usually have such good ideas. This isn't one of your all-time best ones. Come on, let's do a little better."

"You're too important to me to let you do that."

"You're too good a friend. I don't want to see you hurt."

"You have a really good brain. Use it to think of something that won't get us grounded for the rest of our lives."

"Hey, I really like you. I want us to be able to stay friends. If we got caught, then our parents wouldn't let us visit each other."

9. A BETTER IDEA

You can always quickly suggest something else to do—something better—that won't get you and your friend into trouble. You must suggest the alternative with excitement and energy, as if offering an invitation your friend would be crazy to turn down. *A better idea is using positive peer pressure*. Some better ideas include:

"Hey, I've got a good idea! Let's go _____ (to my house to get a soft drink, listen to my new album, visit a friend, see what's on TV, etc.)."

"Why don't we _____ (fill in the blank with a hobby or activity you are involved in that could include your friend, such as "shoot some baskets," "play some football," "look at a new fashion magazine," "practice this new dance I learned.")

There are hundreds of things you could think of to do instead of getting into trouble if you use your imagination. Once you've suggested a *better idea*, it is important that you try to put it into action, possibly leading your friend away from trouble as well.

10. RETURN THE CHALLENGE

When a friend is really pressuring you, maybe even acting hostile, you may have to get tough. When ignoring, making jokes or excuses, or just saying no won't work, it is probably time to *return the challenge*. If you have played tennis, your goal when a partner serves the ball to you is to smash that ball back. *Return the challenge* is similar—you throw your friend's challenge right back. This does not involve physically fighting your friend. It does involve quick thinking so that you can confront your friend with words. This technique is best put to use when your friend is taunting you, saying that he or she will not be your friend if you don't go along, and if your friend is calling you names like "chicken," "scared" and "loser." The most common mistake people make when confronted by such a challenge is to become too defensive: when you, like most people, are called "chicken," your first response is "No I'm not!" Of course, the peer's next response is "OK, prove it!" Then you stomp off with your friend to "show" him or her. Your friend just controlled *you*! Becoming defensive and saying "I am not" backs you right into a corner with no way out. Don't give your friend a chance to say "Prove it." Let's look at other ways to respond.

When a peer accuses you with "I thought you were my friend!", several possible comebacks are:

"Yes, I am your best friend; and that's why I'm not going to do this with you."

"If you were my friend, then you wouldn't be trying to talk me into doing something that I don't want to do."

"With friends like you, who needs enemies? If you were really my friend, you'd stop trying to push me around."

"If you were my friend, you wouldn't be so bossy."

And of course, a more stinging comeback could always be: "Who said you were my friend?"

When the friend taunts you with "Chicken!", "Are you scared?", or the like, there are lots of comebacks. *Remember*: These are suggestions you can choose from—examples of things you *could* say.

"Thanks, I'm glad you noticed. I'm so proud of it."

"So?"

"What's wrong with chickens?"

"Yeah, I am. Anybody smart would be."

"Big deal. I'd rather be a chicken than a turkey like you."

"It takes one to know one."

"Thanks. I'm glad you noticed."

"If I'm the chicken, then you're the egg."

"I know you are, but what am I?"

"I'd rather be a chicken than a jail bird."

Just walk away, flapping your arms like a chicken.
You are communicating to your friends that they are not worth being taken seriously.

"I'd rather be a chicken than a dead duck."

"Are you looking in a mirror?"

Pretend to pluck a feather from your arm, hand it to your friend, and just walk away.

A favorite way to handle the pressuring line of "Are you chicken?" is to toss the "hot potato" right back to your friend. You can use your peer's comments to taunt him or her right back. If you are called "chicken," you could answer:

"Scared to do it by yourself?"

If the peer answers "No," you could say: "Prove it!" as you walk away. If the peer answers "I guess so," you follow up with suggesting a better idea. This response is a good one to stop your friend's teasing! It can even be delivered to a group using the phrase, "You mean you have to *always* have me along? I told you I'm not interested! You all have fun—I hope you don't get into trouble!"

HOW TO SAY IT

You have read *what* to say in a pressure situation, now let's talk about *how* to say it. The way you look when you say these things really does speak louder than the words. The PPR responses are highly effective, but their effect depends upon the way you deliver them. You must look and sound confident and in control, as if you mean what you say.

To look confident, firm, and in control you must "stand tall." This involves sitting, standing, or walking with your back straight. Try not to look passive and scared by gesturing nervously, slouching, or having your head bent down. When you refuse your friend's suggestion—with whatever words—you should face him and maintain eye contact. This again makes you look serious about what you are saying. You shouldn't look mad, just in control! Even if you do not feel confident inside, you can appear confident and bluff your friend. You must look stronger than your pressuring friend. If you appear frightened (even though you might be), move backwards, or shuffle around nervously, your friend will just pressure you more, thinking you might give in.

In order to sound confident, you should speak in a firm and steady voice, not too soft or mumbling. Normally, you should not shout at your friend, because this could start an argument. You don't want to sound undecided by saying things like "I don't *think* so," "We *better* not," "*What* if we get caught?" All of these statements imply that you are open to more pressure.

Also, apply the Thirty Second Rule: start trying to get out of the situation within thirty seconds (or less). This keeps you from being influenced into going along or getting into an argument or fight. More time gives your friend the opportunity to increase the pressure. Avoid debating with your friend and talking too long! However you phrase your no, do so *no more than two times*. After that second no, you should end the discussion by changing the subject, if your friend will allow it, or if necessary just *walk away* from the scene.

For example:

"Let's talk about something else."

"I'm leaving."

"I am not going to talk about this any more." Or just turn your back and walk away.

Do not give your friend the opportunity to persuade you! At first this may be hard for you to do, but it is important to *get the friend off the subject* or *get yourself away* from the friend.

Obviously not all of these responses are right for *you*. Everybody has a different way of dealing with friends. Which work best for you?

4.

PPR

IN

ACTION

(LIGHTS, CAMERA, ACTION!)

Sean and Jeremy have stopped after school at a convenience store to buy soft drinks. They both have just enough money for the drinks and are in the store choosing the one they want.

In a low and excited voice, Sean nudges Jeremy and says, "Hey, I've got an idea." (Jeremy **Checks Out the Scene**, hears potential trouble in the way Sean is talking and immediately puts himself on the alert.) Sean continues, "I'll give you the money for my drink, you go up and pay the clerk for our drinks, and I'll get us both a candy bar. What kind of candy do you want?" While listening, Jeremy asks himself "Is this trouble?" He answers yes and decides the risks aren't worth it. After taking only a moment to think, while looking at the row of sodas, he replies, "No, I'm not into stealing; I don't want to." **(Just say no.)**

Sean gets upset and sharply replies, "Are you chicken or something?"

Jeremy responds, "Are you scared to do it by yourself?" **(Return the challenge.)**

This surprises Sean, who hesitates for a moment and then slowly says, "No-o-o."

Jeremy comes back with "Prove it." (Continuing to **Return the challenge**.)

Immediately, Jeremy leaves his friend inside the store and rides his bicycle toward home **(Leave)**. Jeremy acts as if he has something more interesting to do and soon is surprised to find Sean trying to catch up with him.

Jeremy not only saved himself from potential trouble, but also helped his friend avoid illegal activity. Did you notice that Jeremy had to use a total of three PPR responses to get out of this particular peer pressure situation? Jeremy not only chose good responses, but he also got out of the situation quickly, so his friend didn't have time to continue working on him. Also, he was smart to walk out of the store, because if he had gone up to the clerk to buy his own soft drink, Sean might have misunderstood Jeremy's action to mean that he was going along with him. Or if Sean had stolen the candy with Jeremy still in the store, he might have tried to blame Jeremy in order to get himself out of trouble. Jeremy handled this situation quite confidently.

Kitty was invited to spend Saturday night with her girlfriend, Maria. They had pizza and stayed up late to watch a good movie. The movie ended at midnight, and since neither of them was tired, they tried to decide what to do next. Suddenly Maria said, "Hey, I've got a great idea. I heard there are some guys down the street that are having a party. Why don't we sneak out and walk down to their house and knock on the window? We could just talk to them for a few minutes and be back home real quick. My parents are asleep, and I know they won't wake up. Come on, let's go."

(Kitty recognizes that this is potential trouble when she asks herself: "Is this trouble?" She realizes she must act quickly while being careful not to anger her good friend.)

Kitty replies, "No, I really don't want to. It could be dangerous walking outside this late at night." **(Just say no.)**

Maria interrupts her: "It's only a few houses down; don't make such a big deal out of this. Besides, I was the one who invited you over. I thought you were my friend."

(Kitty hears a peer pressure line and knows a good reply.) Kitty says, "Maria, if you were my friend, you wouldn't try to make me do something that I'm not interested in doing. I don't know any of those boys, and don't want to go walking around this late. Besides, we're not dressed! I've got to get up early tomorrow. My mom is going to take me shopping. Let's go to the kitchen and finish off the lemonade and then go to sleep." (Here Kitty used two PPR techniques— **Excuses** and **Better idea**.)

Her friend Maria moans, "Well, it would have been fun, but I'm not going to *make* you go, so let's go get some lemonade."

Again, several different PPR techniques were needed to avoid the trouble, and Kitty was strong enough to be firm with her best friend. It's not always easy to refuse your close friends, but it can be worth it.

It's Saturday afternoon and Nicholas calls up two friends, Juan and Scott, and invites them to go to a movie. Both say yes and Nicholas's mom agrees to drive them. She tells them she will pick them up after the show at the same location. As soon as she drives off Nicholas says, "Oh, good, I'm glad she's gone. This show really doesn't sound very good. Why don't we walk around the mall instead? We can get back to the theatre before Mom comes. She'll never know we didn't go to the show." (Both Juan and Scott realize that their friend is trying to get them to lie to his mother, and recognize that if they get caught, their parents would probably be called, and maybe the next time they are invited to go some place with a friend, their parents would say no.) At first, Juan can't think of anything to say; he hesitates. Scott quickly thinks of a comeback: "Hey, I heard this show is really good. I want to see it. Besides, if we get caught we would be grounded for a month." This gives Juan the strangth to say, "Yeah, I want to see the show, too; after all, that's what we came to do." (Both guys used **Just say no and Act shocked**.)

Scott and Juan both turn, buy their tickets, and walk into the theatre **(Leave)**. Neither of them is surprised to see their friend, Nicholas, follow them into the show. He gripes at them for a minute, but quiets down when the show begins, and becomes involved in watching a good movie.

Scott and Juan used several PPR responses to free themselves from potential trouble, but did not damage their friendship with Nicholas.

Mandy and Anita are sitting in English class. They are supposed to be writing a short report on the chapter that was just read aloud. Mandy is bored and whispers to her friend, "Psst, what are you going to do after school today?" (Anita realizes the teacher has just instructed the class not to talk; this teacher is very strict.)

Anita continues to work on her paper and pretends not to hear her friend **(Ignore)**. Mandy thinks her friend didn't hear her, so she repeats the question a little louder this time. Anita continues to do her work and realizes that the teacher has heard Mandy talking. The teacher looks at Mandy sternly, indicating that she wants her to be quiet. Mandy immediately begins working on her paper and does not attempt to talk anymore in class that day.

Anita avoided the trouble situation here by ignoring her friend. This is the only PPR technique that she could use in this situation, because if she had made any reply, she might have gotten into trouble with the teacher also.

PPR In Action: Now It's Your Turn

Just for fun, take a minute to try out the PPR skills yourself. You'll need a pencil or pen.

You are standing in front of your locker at school, getting your books for your next class. Your friend, Mitzi, rushes up and whispers to you, "Did you finish your math homework last night? I hope so, because I didn't have time to do mine."

1. Check out the scene by looking and listening:
   What clues are there that this is potential trouble?

   _____

   _____

2. What do you think your friend is preparing to ask you?

   _____

3. Is that trouble? Why?

   _____

   _____

4. What could you say or do at this point to keep your friend from asking to borrow your paper?

   _____

   _____

5. What if Mitzi says, "I thought you were my friend. If you were my friend, you'd help me just this one time." How could you respond to that?

_____

_____

_____

Those are some tough questions. How did you do?

If you thought quickly enough in the very beginning, you may have decided either to **Change the subject** or pretend to be in a big hurry and rush to your next class. Either response used at first would have stopped the situation. If for some reason you could not react that quickly, then maybe you could've used some type of comeback like "Boy, that math was really tough. I'm not even sure I have half of it right. I've got to work on it more before class." A nice additional statement could have been "The next time you are having problems with your math, give me a call. We could help each other on the phone." If your friend says "If you were my friend, you'd help me," you can always **Return the challenge** by saying, "If _you_ were _my_ friend, you wouldn't want to risk my getting a zero when I took the time to do my math last night. And like I said, I'd be glad to help you if I can in the future if you will just call me at home after school."

Handling peer pressure is not always easy, but it sure is nice to stay out of trouble!

Here is another peer pressure situation for you to deal with:

You are walking home from school with friends one day. "Have you seen Peter's new girlfriend? What a bozo! She has no personality at all!"

1. Think carefully on this one. What is the trouble situation?

_____

_____

As you are thinking of what to say or do, another friend continues, "Yeah, she's really a creep, and from the style of clothes she wears, you'd think she buys them at a garage sale. No taste at all!"

2. If you add to this discussion by gossiping with your friends, what bad things can happen?

_____

_____

3. What might you say or do in this situation to handle the trouble most effectively?

_____

_____

Gossip and rumors are never easy to deal with or avoid. They go on in most schools every day and cause us all hurt feelings now and then. This is another situation you can choose to be a part of by going along with your friends and saying unkind things about others. That may be the easy way out because it will please your friends at the moment, but in the long run, it can encourage your friends to gossip more and more. There are several PPR techniques that could be tried here, such as **Change the subject, Ignore**, come up with a **Better idea**, or even **Leave**. If you stay with your friends while they gossip, even though you don't say anything at all, they will assume by your silence that you agree with them. If you are really strong, you might stand up for the person they are criticizing by saying something like "Hey, let's not waste our time just gossiping—there are a lot more fun things to do," and then quickly begin talking about something that might interest most of the group.

You have done well with these two examples. Good work!

5.

TOBACCO, ALCOHOL, DRUGS, and SEXUALITY

This is a special section devoted to some very difficult decisions you will probably face at some time in your preteen or teenage years. This section looks at tobacco, alcohol, illegal drugs, and sexuality. Peers may try to convince you that these things are all right and will make you look grown-up. Poor decisions in these areas result in such severe consequences in people's lives that each area deserves individual attention.

USE OF TOBACCO

Many young people think that smoking cigarettes or using smokeless tobacco (snuff and chewing tobacco) makes them look grown-up. This is one area in which kids can learn a lot from grown-ups. If you look around, you will see many grown-ups trying to quit their use of tobacco. And many are having very difficult times doing so because they have a serious addiction developed over many years of use.

Notice that on a package of cigarettes there is a statement from the Surgeon General of the United States, warning you that cigarette smoking is harmful to your health. However, many young people begin smoking to look cool and then develop the desire to continue smoking, which ultimately results in addiction. Research shows that taking up smoking is clearly associated with the early development of coughs, production of phlegm (thick mucus), and shortness of breath upon exercising. Even after smoking more than a few cigarettes a day for only two years, young people who smoke appear considerably less healthy than their non-smoking peers and show some evidence of early obstruction of the air passages. What this means is that young people who smoke are already developing problems in their lungs.

The U.S. Surgeon General has reported cigarette smoking causes 30 percent of all cancer deaths. Lung cancer is drastically increasing in women due to an increase in their smoking. Heart disease brought on by cigarette smoking may prematurely kill 10 percent of the U.S. population. I don't know if tobacco use has damaged the health of any in your family, but it has in mine. My father was forced to retire early after a serious heart attack, and both my mother-in-law and my uncle died of lung cancer. The doctors said smoking caused the problem in each case.

Many young people, especially athletes, are using smokeless tobacco. Unfortunately, many are suffering from cancer of the mouth brought on by their use of snuff or chewing tobacco. Many young people are having to have surgery to remove the cancerous growths from their mouths and faces and suffer disfigurement as a result. If the cancer is not completely removed, it can lead to death. Nine thousand people die from oral cancer every year.

Smoking is a negative peer pressure situation. The main reason young people begin smoking is because their peers do—and that's not a good reason to do *anything*! You need to know the facts so that you can make an informed decision on whether you choose to become a smoker or continue smoking if you already are one.

One of the PPR steps you learned was *weighing both sides*. It let you look at the positive and negative consequences of your choice. Let's use that to help you look logically at the smoking issue.

Negative Effects
Leads to heart disease
Causes lung cancer
Can lead to death
Smells bad
Yellows your teeth and
 fingernails
Causes serious addiction
 to nicotine
Wastes money
Is illegal to buy if
 under age

Positive Effects
Look grown-up to peers
 who smoke
Relaxed feeling

You'll notice there are many negative consequences to smoking, but only two possible positive effects. Also, if you really examine the positive side of smoking, you will notice that it is temporary. The negative effects are permanent. The real way to act grown-up is to act responsibly, and smoking is not acting responsibly.

Which of the ten PPR responses could be effective to avoid smoking with your friends? Remember that you can always **Just say no**. If you are uncomfortable with that response with certain groups of friends, then you can use most of the other techniques, such as **Leave, Make an excuse**, ("I don't feel like it," or "I need to get home now."), **Change the subject, Act shocked, Flattery**, a **Better idea**, or even **Return the challenge**. If your friend is pressuring you hard, ask your friend if he or she is scared to smoke without you! Of course, making a joke also lends itself to getting out of a smoking situation. Some joking lines to avoid smoking could be:

 "No thanks. I'm not into body pollution."
 "No. I don't want any cancer sticks today."
 "Don't want any coffin nails today."

"Uh—uh, not for me. Smoking is the *real* reason
why dinosaurs became extinct."

Remember to look at the *facts* and make a good
decision for yourself. So many people who develop this
addiction later would give anything if they could quit!

USE OF ALCOHOL

Alcohol is one of the more readily available drugs. I bet you didn't know that alcohol is considered a drug. It is a depressant, a drug that slows down the central nervous system. Many people ask why it is legal if it is a drug. In all states there is a certain age under which it is illegal to buy and drink alcohol. The fact of the matter is that alcohol usage in the civilized world began thousands of years ago. It is now so widely accepted that to try to get it totally outlawed would almost be impossible.

The active ingredient in alcohol is a chemical called ethyl alcohol, which taken in large doses is poison to the body. When a person drinks, the liver filters alcohol from the blood stream and eliminates it from the body. The liver can filter about one ounce of alcohol per hour. If someone drinks more than an ounce of alcohol per hour, the person becomes intoxicated—or drunk. Notice the word *toxic* is part of intoxication—and toxic means *poisonous*.

Some statistics about alcohol use in the United States:

- There are roughly 9 million persons who have become problem drinkers.
- Of those problem drinkers 3.3 million are teenagers.
- More than half of all teenage deaths are alcohol or drug related.
- Forty-nine percent of high school students drink in cars, which accounts for part of the 28 thousand people who die as a result of drunk driving every year. (That is more than 60 deaths per day!)

- Another 40 thousand young people suffer serious highway injuries linked to alcohol. (In fact, every five seconds a teenager has an alcohol or drug-related traffic accident.)

People are consuming alcohol at a younger age each year. Today, the average age of those just starting to use alcohol is 12½. Research that shows that the younger a person is when he or she starts to drink alcohol, the greater are the chances that the person will develop into a chronic alcoholic. Alcoholism in adolescence develops very rapidly, with some teenagers becoming alcoholics within six months after taking their first drink.

Look at a list of pros and cons of alcohol usage:

Negative Effects	Positive Effects
Damage to brain and liver cells	Look grown-up to drinking friends
You say things you don't mean or wish you hadn't said	Feel relaxed
Arrest, if bought or used under age or while driving	
Dependence on alcohol to relax	
Alcoholism	
Slurred speech, slowed reflexes	
Expensive	
Impaired thinking	
Nausea, vomiting	
Loss of non-drinking friends	
Hangover	

Again, note that there is a longer list of negative consequences. Again, the positive side effects are temporary—many of the negative effects are not. There are many other things you can do to look grown-up and to relax—get a job, play a musical instrument, exercise, do well on a school assignment, or excel in a hobby.

Any of the ten PPR responses will be helpful to avoid drinking with your friends, including **Just say no** or **Leave, Make an excuse, Change the subject**. Of course, if you are in a one-on-one situation with a friend, you can always **Act shocked** ("I can't believe you would drink. If your parents knew, you'd be grounded the rest of your life!") or you can talk your friend into doing something that is not harmful and is legal, such as "Let's go play this new game I've got," or "I want you to see this new outfit I got." There are also joking ways of avoiding alcohol usage:

> "Oh, darling, I only drink champagne." (If your
> friend happens to have champagne, and brings
> that to you, reply, "Not my year.")
> "I never drink before I'm drunk."
> "I'd rather hang loose than hangover."
> "I might forget where I parked my brain."
> "I probably would barf all over your car. No thanks."
> "Not my brand."
> "I'm allergic. It makes my skin turn green."
> "No booze is good booze."
> "I don't need to loosen up. I just got it together!"

Look at the *facts*. They speak loudly. Having been a counselor for over sixteen years, I have seen firsthand the trouble young people get into because of drinking. I have seen kids get arrested and get into trouble with their parents. Worse yet, I have seen them end up in hospitals because of alcoholism, and even seriously injured or killed because of driving while drinking. My parents' neighbors lost their son on the night of his high school graduation because he was drinking while driving. Five out of the six kids in the car died. It should have been a night for celebration and joy, but it turned into a nightmare because of their poor decisions.

USE OF ILLEGAL DRUGS

In most states drug arrests of young people in their early teens is climbing at an alarming rate. Health problems and car accidents attributed to drug usage are on the increase as well. If you are going to fight drug abuse in your own life, you must know the facts.

Let's concentrate on marijuana, since it is commonly the first drug used by young people. There are over 7 thousand studies that show the harmful physical effects of marijuana. Let's look at a few.

What does marijuana do to the *brain*? It widens the gap between brain cells, thus slowing down the nerve impulses which affect your short-term memory. This is one of the reasons why most young people's grades decline after pot usage has begun. Pot impairs their ability to evaluate situations. During my years with the police department I saw many young people break laws while under the influence of marijuana. Many of these young people would not have made these poor decisions at other times, but they couldn't look at the situation carefully while they were high. Also, driving is impaired for up to 12 hours after smoking only one joint.

What is the effect of marijuana on the *lungs*? Marijuana smoke is more irritating and harmful than cigarette smoke—and we've already seen how harmful cigarette smoke is! Studies show that smoking one joint is more harmful to the lungs than smoking a whole pack of cigarettes! Marijuana can cause precancerous lesions (abnormal changes in cells) in two or three years. It makes lungs more susceptible to emphysema and bronchitis.

What is the effect of marijuana on *blood cells*? It causes a decrease in white cell production which causes interference with the body's ability to fight off infections and disease. You may note that many young people who smoke pot frequently have colds, coughs, and other upper respiratory infections.

Marijuana even affects personality, as users develop the *"amotivational syndrome,"* best described as not caring about anything—such as school grades, following rules or obeying parents. However, users normally cannot see this happening to themselves; they actually think they are accomplishing more instead of less.

Most people don't know that marijuana contains over four hundred different chemicals, of which the best known is *THC*. Because THC likes fat, it is absorbed by organs in the body that have a high fat content, like brain, liver, and reproductive organs. The body can only eliminate THC very slowly, often taking four weeks. THC does its main damage long *after* the person has been high. Users, in fact, are totally unaware of its presence in their bodies! If a person smokes only one joint every month, his or her body is *never* drug free!

Every year more than sixty thousand young people under the age of eighteen require treatment for drug usage. Their average length of treatment, or stay in a rehabilitation center, is 11½ months.

In examining a list of pros and cons about using drugs, the harmful effects are overwhelming. When most drug users are asked why they do drugs, the most common answer is "Because my friends are doing it." Here again, negative peer pressure causes people not to listen to their common sense, and gets them into dangerous situations that they know are extremely serious. Some people will tell you that marijuana makes you feel good. However, you must realize this is a *temporary* and artificial high. This feeling can become addictive, an escape from problems that are going on in day-to-day life; but at some point everyone has to grow up and deal with those problems. Drugs can't make those problems go away.

Some of the negative consequences of marijuana:

- Damage to brain, lungs, liver, and reproductive organs
- Imprisonment, or other actions of the courts (drugs are illegal)
- Loss of friends
- Decrease in energy (users often drop out of sports or hobbies)
- Poor concentration and school performance
- Increase in upper respiratory infections
- Decline in family relationships and increase in arguments
- "I don't care" attitude
- Tolerance develops (you need more of the drug as time goes by to get the same high)
- Waste of money

You can use the ten PPR techniques to avoid drug usage also. If you are really strong, you can **Just say no**. Other responses include **Leave**, tell the person to do it by him or herself because you are not interested, and **Make an excuse** (no time, money or interest). Of course, there are some low-key joking responses that work well here. Your friends know you are saying no, but in a different way:

"I don't smoke grass, just mow it."
"I just popped a few M&Ms, can't handle anymore today!"
"I almost overdosed on marker fumes today in art class. Had enough!"
"Is that a low-tar joint? I only smoke low-tar joints."

You may be asked to use drugs other than marijuana, such as pills, sniffing paint, cocaine, or designer drugs. All of these are extremely harmful; they require a strong no answer if you are asked to use any of them.

"Designer" drugs is a name for drugs made by people in laboratories. They resemble other drugs. "Designer" does *not* mean a reliable brand as it does in clothing. People make these drugs for money, and they don't care who they are sold to or how they might harm people.

A teenage girl was at a convenience store with friends having a soft drink when a group of older kids drove up to buy ice. They were invited to a party by these kids, none of whom they knew. They decided to go to the party, knowing they could always leave if it was too wild. (No one **Checked Out the Scene**— trouble was evident: these kids were loud, they smelled like alcohol, they were buying ice, and they invited total strangers to their party.) The party was crowded and noisy, and people there were drunk, but the girl and her friends decided to stay anyway. After a while they decided to leave, but could not find the girl. They thought she might have gone to the car, so they started for the parking lot and found her unconscious in the street. They quickly drove her home and apologized to her parents, thinking she was drunk.

Her mother was worried. The girl was dirty, her clothes were torn, her pulse was rapid, and she just barely smelled of alcohol. The mother called the hospital emergency room, and the hospital said to bring her in. Tests revealed that her blood pressure was very high; she had probably taken the designer drug, Ecstasy. Tests also showed that she had been raped. The girl had no memory from the moment she took one drink at the party until she woke up in the hospital.

Please realize there are no good drugs. Have the courage to make a logical, self-protective decision based on the facts.

SEXUALITY

This section is intended to provide you with factual information so that when you have to make decisions about your sexuality, you'll make logical instead of emotional ones. Many people decide to begin sexual activity for the wrong reasons—curiosity; they feel everyone else is doing it; they are trying to keep a boy or girl friend; they don't know what to say to a date; or as women, they want to be "fulfilled," and as males, they want to prove they are men.

Many people decide to have sex when they think they are in love. Most will be in love many times during their lives, and each relationship will have its own special qualities. But if you have sex with everyone you think you love, you will probably have a large number of sexual partners. Many boys and girls who do this develop reputations for being "loose" or "wild." Unfortunately, it then becomes difficult to know if people are dating you because they really like you or because you are sexually active with a number of people.

Here are some facts about teenage sexual activity:

- Almost one of every ten teenage girls in the United States becomes pregnant each year.
- Within six months after becoming sexually active, half of all teenage girls become pregnant.
- Most teenagers do not use contraceptives (birth control methods) until they have been sexually active for about nine months—most just hope that they won't get pregnant.

- In 1981, 1.1 million teenagers became pregnant, 75 percent unintentionally. Of those pregnancies, 537 thousand resulted in births, 434 thousand in abortions, and 151 thousand in miscarriages.
- Eight out of ten pregnant teenagers dropped out of school.
- Six out of ten who married were divorced within five years.

If you think you are going to be the only one that does not have sex with your boy or girl friends, you are not alone. In fact, at least 50 percent of girls and 40 percent of boys are still virgins at their high school graduation. Don't let the bragging of others influence you or make you feel out of it. Be careful when you are watching TV, listening to rock music, and reading magazines, because they can confuse you and make you feel that everyone spends his or her entire life partying. That is not so.

After a relationship breaks up (and most will at some time during your teenage years, since it is very unlikely that you will find your marriage partner during those years), people feel sad and lonely. Those are normal feelings. But if a person has dated someone for a while, had sex with him or her, and then broken up, a lot of times the person feels used. This emotion can be much stronger and more difficult for people to deal with; it damages our self-esteem.

Some of the pros and cons about teenage sexual activity are:

NEGATIVE EFFECTS	POSITIVE EFFECTS
Unwanted pregnancy	A way to try to "hold onto" a boy or girl friend
STD (sexually transmitted diseases)	Feeling of being loved
Requires lots of decisions: birth control method, how to deal with your parents, plans should you become pregnant, etc.	Feeling older, more mature
Decrease in casual, friendly dating and an emphasis placed on sex during dating	
Feeling used after break-up	

Of course you want to keep your boy or girl friend and to feel loved. There are other ways to do this without being sexually active and risking the sometimes severe consequences of that kind of activity. Keeping friends requires many kinds of attention, such as dressing nicely; buying them small, thoughtful gifts; buying tickets for an event you know they'll like; being on time for dates; and having interesting conversations.

Pregnancy is a risk of sexual involvement. It can complicate not only your life, but also that of your friend, your friend's parents, and the life of the unborn child. If you become a parent right now, could you support a child, complete your education, *and* have time for fun? Not likely. You have your life ahead of you. There is no need to rush this decision or take risks.

In the time it takes you to read this sentence, a young American man or woman between the ages of 15 and 25 will become infected with a sexually transmitted disease (STD). Not only do we have to worry about pregnancy as a consequence of sex, but also have to be concerned about over 20 diseases that are frequently spread by sexual contact. Over 10 million new cases are expected this year!

And AIDS has already become a major health problem in this country. The World Health Organization estimates that 5 million to 10 million people already have been infected with the virus. There is no cure and most of those who acquire this disease, which is spread mainly through sexual contact as well as by drug users sharing needles, will die within 2 years!

You can avoid sexual activity by avoiding situations that will offer opportunity. For example, don't go to your friend's house when you know there is no adult there; plan activities when you go out on a date instead of just driving around; date in groups; go to indoor theatres instead of drive-ins; and think up some interesting subjects to talk about ahead of time.

Some of you reading this may already be sexually active. I seriously hope that you reconsider this decision due to the many risks that you are taking. Should you decide not to change your mind, then please use condoms. Don't rely on your partner to take care of this, it's your responsibility. They can reduce the chance of pregnancy and disease, but are *not* 100% effective. Nor can they protect you from the emotional risks that you are taking. Please remember that the safest way to avoid all of these risks is to not become sexually involved at all (abstinence). You have a lifetime to become sexually involved—why not wait to a safer time which would include two mature, financially secure people within a marriage?

If your boy or girl friend says "If you really loved me. you would go to bed with me," you can use the **Return the challenge** response by saying, "If *you* really loved *me*, you wouldn't be pressuring me to do something I'm not ready for"—*and they wouldn't*. Try not to be embarrassed or shy about standing up for yourself!

6.

SUMMARY

I hope this book has helped you examine how you make decisions and what direction you want to take in your life. You *can* be anyone you want to be, and do anything you want unless poor decisions cause you to get into enough trouble to endanger your future. Take another look at Life's Decision-Making Road on page 23, and remember, you are planning your life out *now*. Which direction will you choose?

Everyone really wants to choose a direction which lets him or her make good decisions, stay out of trouble, gain the trust of others, and be successful. Everyone wants his or her lives to work out. But letting peers encourage you in the wrong direction can take that away from you. Don't let it happen. Use peer pressure reversal!

Everyday in my work I hear of another situation which led someone to get hurt or into trouble. Negative peer pressure can get people in all kinds of minor and serious trouble. But now you've read and learned more about peer pressure, and you can see that it can be prevented. It's nice to know you can stay out of trouble *and* have lots of friends. With the skill of peer pressure reversal, you can be a winner! My best to you.

Sharon Scott is available in the following capacities:

— Speaker for youth or parent groups
— Workshop leader for professional training
— Keynote presentation at conferences
— Consultant to school districts, counseling agencies, law enforcement settings, etc.

For more information please write:

Sharon Scott, L.P.C., President
Scott and Associates
2709 Woods Lane
Garland, TX 75044-2807

Other titles by Sharon Scott:

• Peer Pressure Reversal: An Adult Guide to Developing a Responsible Child
• Positive Peer Groups
• When to Say Yes! And Make More Friends
• Too Smart for Trouble

Available from:

Human Resource Development Press
22 Amherst Road
Amherst, MA 01002

1-800-822-2801 (outside Massachusetts)
(413) 253-3488 (inside Massachusetts)